Cross-currents in French Defense and U.S. Interests

Cross-currents in French Defense and U.S. Interests

By Leo G. Michel

Institute for National Strategic Studies
Strategic Perspectives, No. 10

Series Editor: Nicholas Rostow

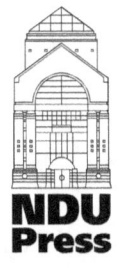

National Defense University Press
Washington, D.C.
April 2012

First printing, April 2012

For current publications of the Institute for National Strategic Studies, please go to the National Defense University Web site at: www.ndu.edu/inss.

Contents

Executive Summary

France is the only European ally—except for the United Kingdom (UK)—that regards its military capabilities, operational performance, and defense industry as vital levers to exert global influence. While the French believe strongly in their need to preserve "strategic independence," they see new challenges in the evolving international security environment that will oblige them to accept greater cooperation with others, even in areas once considered too sensitive to discuss. Although some French strategists remain uncomfortable with the notion of closer defense ties with the United States, others ask whether there might be a greater danger ahead: specifically, if Europe's strength dissipates as America "rebalances" toward the Asia-Pacific region, where does France turn to find capable and willing partners to protect its security interests?

The Libyan conflict in 2011 brought to light many of the cross-currents that are shaping French defense policy. French leaders are proud of their military's performance in Libya, which many view as having validated President Nicolas Sarkozy's decision in early 2009 on France's return to full participation in North Atlantic Treaty Organization (NATO) military structures. But the conflict also exposed Europe's continuing dependence on U.S. military capabilities, reinforced France's lack of confidence in Germany and the European Union as serious military partners, and increased its determination to improve defense cooperation with the United Kingdom.

Despite some downsizing, France has resisted the dramatic cuts in defense spending and capabilities under way elsewhere in Europe. If Sarkozy wins the presidential election on May 6, 2012, he can be expected to continue many elements of the transformation strategy launched by his government's June 2008 *White Book on Defense and National Security*. If the Socialist Party challenger, François Hollande, wins, he will reassure leaders at the NATO Summit in Chicago (May 20–21, 2012) that France will maintain its nuclear deterrent and participation in NATO military structures. But reductions in the defense budget are likely whether Sarkozy or Hollande wins.

There will be opportunities for expanded U.S.-French and perhaps U.S.-UK-French defense cooperation under a Sarkozy or Hollande administration. But Paris and Washington will need to manage tensions related to their respective defense industries. For the United States, more is at stake than the health of the French defense establishment. France's policies, capabilities, and operational commitments can play an important role in shaping those of many other Europeans. By working even more closely with its oldest ally, the United States can help ensure the credibility and effectiveness of the Alliance as a whole.

Changing Strategic Context: View from Paris

"Europe is disarming while the [rest of the] world rearms," Admiral Édouard Guillaud, France's chief of defense, told French parliamentarians in October 2011. "This is not something new. But if this trend were to continue, it would have serious consequences for our future as a power that can count in world affairs."[1] Guillaud's warning reflects a strong current of strategic thought among many influential French officials and nongovernmental experts. In their view, France today is a leading military power inside Europe and in nearby regions. Moreover, it is the only European ally—except for the United Kingdom—that regards its military capabilities, operational performance, and defense industry as vital levers to exert global influence. However, the French see mounting challenges in the evolving international security environment.

A February 2012 interministerial study highlights areas of particular concern.[2] For example, according to the study:

- Since the 2008 *White Book on Defense and National Security* (White Book), numerous vulnerabilities and threats have intensified, particularly in the areas of cyber security, weapons proliferation (notably involving Iran), and risks to the global commons.[3]

- Upheavals in the Arab world—which, the study acknowledges, were a "strategic surprise"—will take years to play out and will permanently alter regional balances. The Mediterranean region, part of the "arc of crisis" identified by the White Book, is now "at the heart of [French] strategic interests."[4]

- The continuing international financial and economic turbulence, including European sovereign debt problems, "constitute a radically new element" that accelerates the progressive shift of the "strategic center of gravity" toward Asia, especially China and India.[5]

- While the United States is expected to remain the "single overarching global power" until at least 2025, it is reaching the end of its post-9/11 emphasis on a "global war on terror" and turning away from large scale stabilization operations. Moreover, "the progressive shift of U.S. interest toward Asia contributes to a relative decline in Europe's strategic importance within global American strategy."[6]

- Despite the death of Osama bin Laden and reported weakening of al Qaeda's base in the Afghanistan-Pakistan region, terrorist groups—notably al Qaeda–affiliated groups in the Maghreb, Arabian Peninsula, and Horn of Africa—remain a strategic concern. France remains "a favorite target" for such groups, who might seek to mount a major attack in Europe involving nonconventional weapons.[7]

The interministerial study does not propose specific modifications to existing defense policy and capabilities. It suggests, however, that the new White Book (to be prepared by the next government in late 2012) will need to address tensions among France's level of ambition, budgetary resources, and ability to work with others on terms acceptable to Paris. The study asserts, for example, that "maintaining strategic independence remains a key issue for France," but later states that French policy must evolve toward greater multilateral cooperation, including within European frameworks and North Atlantic Treaty Organization (NATO) military structures.[8]

Determining the right balance between independence and cooperation will not be an easy task. Indeed, many French experts worry that their country will be unable to maintain its global rank in the coming years absent significantly expanded defense cooperation with other Europeans and, in some areas, with the United States. However, the somber economic outlook for the European Union (EU)—where cumulative gross domestic product (GDP) is predicted to shrink by 0.5 percent in 2012, in contrast with a predicted 6 percent growth in the Brazilian, Russian, Indian, and Chinese economies—has fueled increasing French pessimism regarding European defense efforts as well.[9] Moreover, while some French strategists remain uncomfortable with the notion of closer defense ties with the United States, since they traditionally have looked to reduce the U.S. influence over European security affairs, others ask whether there might be a greater danger ahead: specifically, if Europe's strength dissipates as America "rebalances" toward the Asia-Pacific region, where does France turn to find capable and willing partners to protect its security interests?[10]

Hence, French defense leaders must navigate amid a number of strong cross-currents. There is little doubt anymore that their country must turn toward greater cooperation with others, even in areas formerly considered too sensitive to discuss. But for the French, finding the right mix of partners and areas of cooperation has become a much more complicated affair than they anticipated just a few years ago.

French Defense Capabilities: Major Trends

When Nicolas Sarkozy unveiled the White Book, few experts were predicting the financial and economic crisis about to engulf the United States and, soon thereafter, Europe. So far, French authorities have resisted pressures to cut defense budgets as deeply as their British and

German counterparts, who have reduced their budgets by approximately 8 and 14 percent, respectively, over the next 4 to 5 years. However, some belt-tightening is already evident.

After rising from €30 billion (excluding pensions) in 2008 to almost €33 billion in 2009, France's overall defense spending returned to €31 billion in 2011.[11] In 2011, defense "equipment" costs (including acquisition, infrastructure, research and development, and equipment maintenance) accounted for €16 billion, and "non-equipment" costs (mainly personnel salaries and logistics costs associated with overseas operations) accounted for €15 billion.[12] Under current plans, a small increase in equipment expenditures will take place during 2012, mainly to compensate for inflation. Overall, defense expenditures represent approximately 1.7 percent of the country's GDP, placing France about midway between the 2.4 percent of GDP figure for the United Kingdom and the comparable 1.2 percent figure for Germany.[13]

While the pace of modernization programs has been slower than anticipated by the White Book, France has made significant efforts to maintain its "full spectrum" of capabilities. Several major new weapons systems (or additions to existing systems) have entered into service since 2008 or are expected to do so during 2012. On the conventional side, these include multirole combat aircraft, multirole and attack helicopters, more capable armored vehicles and mobile artillery, advanced infantry protection and communications systems, air defense frigates and missile systems, a new multimission frigate, and a third *Mistral*-class amphibious force projection and command ship. On the nuclear side, these include a fourth ballistic missile submarine, more capable submarine-launched ballistic missiles, and nuclear armed air-to-ground missiles.

The White Book emphasized the importance of space and intelligence, surveillance, and reconnaissance capabilities. Since 2008, the French have established a joint space command and sought to improve cooperation among the intelligence services. They will begin development this year of a new electromagnetic and optical satellite (the Multinational Space-based Imaging System for Surveillance, Reconnaissance, and Observation, or, MUSIS) as well as a prototype ballistic missile warning radar.

The White Book's plan to reduce defense personnel is largely on track. Since 2009, some 15 regiments and battalions, 13 army headquarters, and 4 air bases have been closed. Total military personnel will be further reduced from its 2009 level of 242,000 to approximately 225,000 by the end of 2012. The army, now at about 124,000 soldiers, likely will absorb slightly larger cuts than the air force (52,000 personnel) or navy (39,000 personnel).[14]

The White Book hinted at a reduction in the number of French military personnel overseas, but did not set any specific target. In fact, the decline in overseas presence has been significant. In late 2007, some 14,000 military were engaged in several operational theaters across

Europe, Africa, the Middle East, and South Asia under various NATO, EU, or United Nations (UN) mandates or bilateral arrangements. In addition, some 24,000 served as "sovereignty" or "presence" forces in several French overseas departments and in francophone Africa.[15] As of January 2012, the comparable figures were 7,300 and 13,000, respectively, reflecting in part drawdowns from operations in the Balkans and Côte d'Ivoire.[16] In this context, one development deserves special mention: in 2009, France established a military installation in the United Arab Emirates (UAE) where some 650 personnel support French air force and naval operations in the Persian Gulf region, specialized training for French army units, and French defense cooperation with the UAE military.

In support of these capabilities and deployed forces, France maintains some of the world's largest, most diverse, and most technologically advanced defense industries. According to the interministerial study, the defense sector includes more than 4,000 companies and 165,000 jobs.[17] France ranks fourth worldwide in arms exports (behind the United States, United Kingdom, and Russia), with over €8 billion in orders in 2009; in some cases, these sales are critically important to making advanced systems affordable for its own military.[18] Moreover, defense investments, particularly in advanced technologies, have synergistic benefits for French civilian markets. Hence, issues related to defense industrial cooperation, competition, and arms exports receive close attention from politicians across the ideological spectrum.

France and NATO: Coming to Terms

In August 2007, when Sarkozy first stated his intent to deepen French involvement in NATO, even his staunch opponents did little to mobilize large-scale protests against this break with traditional Gaullist policy. By April 2009, when NATO heads of state and government formally welcomed France's return to full participation in NATO military structures, the debate over Sarkozy's decision within the French political class had largely subsided.[19] Today, the rapprochement with NATO seems irreversible.

According to knowledgeable French officials, Sarkozy had two overriding goals in mind with his decision on NATO: to solidify U.S.-French relations, which still bore scars from the deep divide between Washington and Paris over the invasion of Iraq in 2003; and to allay suspicions elsewhere in Europe (as well as in the United States) that French initiatives to strengthen the EU Common Security and Defense Policy (CSDP) aimed, in fact, to promote the European Union as an alternative to NATO.[20] Beyond these goals, however, Sarkozy and his top advisors reportedly provided little guidance to defense and foreign ministry officials regarding the specific policies, priorities, and organizational changes that French representatives should pursue within the Alliance. According to a former French government official, this situation allowed those who were displeased with the president's decision, notably in the foreign ministry, to resist or delay aspects of its practical implementation.[21]

Still, the French military's return to full participation in NATO structures beginning in April 2009 proceeded relatively smoothly. Previously, only around 200 French officers and non-commissioned officers (NCOs) worked with NATO staffs and agencies, mostly in liaison positions. As of April 2009, NATO procedures allowed France to nominate some 1,250 officers and NCOs to serve within "integrated" positions, including several top-level posts. According to former French government insiders, military authorities in Paris made a conscious decision to advance some of their best regarded officers for Alliance approval. Moreover, these authorities decided to demonstrate their intent to be team players by offering personnel to work in a wide range of NATO directorates.

As a result of this process, Air Force Chief of Staff General Stéphane Abrial was named as Supreme Commander, Allied Command Transformation (ACT), becoming the first European to lead one of NATO's two Supreme Commands. Like Abrial, a dozen other French general officers who assumed prominent NATO posts had previous experience working in Alliance headquarters and/or operations. (The French also credit American military leaders with demonstrating a strong will to help Abrial succeed. Those American officers included Abrial's predecessor at ACT, Marine General James Mattis, who had served concurrently as commander of U.S. Joint Forces Command, and Admiral James Stavridis, who is Supreme Allied Commander Europe.)

Senior French military officers, governmental officials, and nongovernmental experts cite a range of benefits from their country's return to full participation in NATO military structures. However, they do not necessarily agree on how to assess the impact of that increased participation in any specific instance. For example:

- By and large, French military officers and civilian officials contend that they have gained greater influence over the strategic direction of, and operational planning for, NATO missions where French forces are or likely to be heavily committed. NATO's involvement in Libya is widely acknowledged as a high point for such influence, although—as discussed later—it also fueled French concerns about the efficacy of NATO military structures. But opinions vary considerably regarding the International Security Assistance Force (ISAF) in Afghanistan. In particular, some retired senior officers, politicians, and nongovernmental experts complain that France has had relatively limited ability to shape NATO's approach in Afghanistan, given the much larger American commitment there.

- The expanded French presence at ACT—in addition to Abrial, some 100 French officers and NCOs serve in the 600-person command, which is based in Norfolk, Virginia—is seen in a particularly positive light from Paris's perspective. French officers believe it has begun to instill a heightened sense of European responsibility for ACT's role regarding capability development, doctrine, and training; in their view, this has been critical to maintaining and, in some areas, improving ACT's effectiveness following the U.S. decision to dis-establish U.S. Joint Forces Command in August 2011. In addition, the prominent French presence has attracted greater interest in ACT on the part of European defense industry representatives. And NATO officials, as well as government officials in Paris, credit Abrial with advancing pragmatic, albeit informal, cooperation with the European Defense Agency (EDA), which serves as the focal point for capabilities development efforts under EU auspices.

- France's upgraded participation in NATO structures has brought other tangible, albeit indirect, benefits. Senior British officials have explicitly linked the French move to London's readiness to expand bilateral defense cooperation under the November 2010 Lancaster House treaties (see discussion below). Abrial's periodic visits to Washington for meetings on NATO issues with U.S. officials, Members of Congress (and their staffs), and think tank experts have improved their understanding of French contributions to the Alliance. And Abrial's relationship with senior American and French officials has proven useful, on occasion, in facilitating bilateral contacts between Washington and Paris.

For most French defense experts, the costs associated with their country's changed role in NATO have not been onerous, despite dire predictions by some of Sarkozy's critics. Due in large part to NATO's decisions in 2009–2010 to reform and downsize its command structure, France never filled its theoretical quota of 1,250 positions; with full implementation of those reforms over the next year or so, French participation will stabilize at around 925 military personnel. While the assignment of hundreds of officers and NCOs to NATO structures created disruptions in certain headquarters and units based in France and accelerated reductions in overseas military attaché offices, these reportedly have had a minimal impact on operations and readiness. Moreover, the supplemental financial costs associated with increased French participation in NATO—these involve, for the most part, overseas living allowances and somewhat higher contributions to NATO common military and infrastructure budgets—seem relatively modest. According to French military experts, these supplemental costs have risen for various reasons since 2009, but they are expected to stabilize at around €75 million annually by 2020, which represents less than 3 percent of current overall defense spending.[22]

Nevertheless, a few French politicians and commentators occasionally revive past claims that France's international stature will suffer as a result of its expanded participation in NATO, which they view as part of Sarkozy's alleged "alignment" with U.S. policy. Some assert that once the French return to NATO structures was decided, the Sarkozy government quickly lost interest in promoting CSDP. They also assert that, despite reservations in parts of Sarkozy's government and military, he became more susceptible to U.S. pressure to increase French forces in ISAF. Others suggest that Paris has somehow lost influence in Moscow, Beijing, and in other capitals of emerging powers due to its greater involvement in NATO, although they have not advanced any credible evidence for such assertions.

Some respected retired flag officers and nongovernmental think tank experts, who are not ideologically opposed to NATO or closer cooperation with the United States, voice more long-term concerns. They worry that if France puts too much emphasis on military cooperation within the Alliance context, it risks developing the same dependency on U.S. capabilities and political leadership—and, with it, a concomitant erosion of their country's "will to fight"—that they decry as all too prevalent among their fellow Europeans. They also worry that if France invests in NATO common assets to the detriment of its national forces, it might find that those common assets are not available in a crisis due to objections by one or more of the other Allies.

Libya: A Wake-up Call

France's prominent role in the Libyan uprising that eventually ousted Muammar Qadhafi in 2011 has been an important catalyst in framing the defense debate. In public, French officials, parliamentarians, and the media have praised their military's performance in Libya as part of an interim U.S.-UK-French "coalition of the willing" (Operation *Odyssey Dawn*) and NATO's follow-on Operation *Unified Protector*. Beneath the surface, however, the Libyan experience has deepened widespread concerns within French defense circles regarding European capabilities, including their own.

On the positive side of the ledger, according to Guillaud, France contributed some 40 fixed-wing combat aircraft, 20 attack helicopters, and 10 combat and support ships to the Libyan operations, and French pilots conducted 25 percent of the air sorties, including 20 percent of strikes involving fixed-wing aircraft and 90 percent of helicopter strikes.[23] (Although the French were not among the top "bomb droppers" during the early stages of the campaign, according to

NATO experts, they rose to become a leader in this category during the last 2 months of Operation *Unified Protector*.[24]) For French armament officials, the operation confirmed the technical capabilities and reliability of their strike, sensor, and helicopter protection systems.[25]

Moreover, several well-placed French experts believe their forces generally outperformed the British in terms of operational flexibility, effectiveness, and—particularly in helicopter attacks—willingness to take risks to engage Libyan targets.[26] French officers are particularly proud that their government was willing—and able—to conduct the first strike of the campaign on March 19, which was aimed at stopping Qadhafi's forces outside rebel-held Benghazi without coordinating with their British (or American) coalition partners; for that attack, French forces could operate "autonomously," using their national airborne warning and control aircraft, aerial refuelers, and strike aircraft. As one senior French officer commented, "Before Libya, we always measured ourselves against the British. Libya, to our surprise, showed that we are ahead of them in many ways."[27]

On the other hand, the Libyan operation underscored French and, more broadly, European reliance on U.S. strike assets (including cruise missiles and specialized aircraft), "enablers" (such as aerial tankers, intelligence, surveillance, and reconnaissance systems, and targeting experts), and—for some Allies—transfers of precision-guided munitions to defeat what many considered a third-rate adversary. Although some French officials privately have speculated that an exclusively European coalition of the willing could have managed the Libyan operation without U.S. participation, their view is contested by French military analysts who point to the critical role of U.S. enablers in sustaining the pace, intensity, and accuracy of the air campaign. For example, the more than 30 U.S. tanker aircraft committed to the operation allowed allied and partner aircraft to increase greatly their time on station—an especially important factor in permitting the effective targeting of mobile Libyan units and fixed military sites. Together, these enablers greatly reduced the inherent risks to European, Canadian, and other partner forces, minimized the number of Libyan civilian casualties, and thus prevented Qadhafi from exploiting cracks in the NATO-led coalition as the conflict dragged on.

The Libyan operation also validated Sarkozy's decision to rejoin NATO military structures, according to a wide range of French officials, politicians, and experts. Initially, France resisted a leading role for NATO for a variety of mainly political considerations. Some French officials were concerned that Germany, following its abstention on UN Security Council Resolution 1973 authorizing member states to take "all necessary measures" to protect Libyan civilians, might not join the consensus necessary to approve a NATO mission.[28] French officials also worried about opposition from Turkey, which had bridled at Sarkozy's early efforts to take center stage in rallying the international community to stop Qadhafi's attacks on civilians. And many in Paris anticipated a strong negative reaction among Arab states to NATO involvement.

Some French officials privately acknowledge that, in retrospect, Paris had underestimated NATO's ability, for several reasons, to coalesce quickly around a decision to take action in Libya. The insistence by American and British officials on a rapid transfer of command and control responsibilities from their ad hoc coalition with the French (Operation *Odyssey Dawn*) to NATO drew strong support from Norway, Denmark, Belgium, Italy, and Canada; these Allies were prepared to join strike operations, but only within a NATO context. As the number of Allies prepared to approve a NATO operation increased, Germany and Turkey concluded (for different reasons) that they had little incentive to block consensus, especially since they were not obliged to participate militarily in Operation *Unified Protector*. Moreover, three Arab states—Qatar, UAE, and Jordan—proved both willing and able to contribute aircraft and other military assets to the NATO operation, which received broad political support from other Arab League members, as well. Meanwhile, Sweden—a member of the Partnership for Peace that has participated in NATO-led operations in the Balkans and Afghanistan—quickly decided to contribute aircraft to Operation *Unified Protector*, albeit in an intelligence, surveillance, and reconnaissance role rather than in direct strikes.

And some French officials concede that despite its shortcomings, the NATO command structure proved an adaptable "skeleton" that Allies can reinforce relatively quickly with specialized capabilities. They cite, as an example, the rapid influx of American (with some British and French) intelligence and targeting specialists to a NATO installation outside Naples, Italy, to handle the complex demands of continuous air operations.

In Search of Capable and Reliable European Partners

Even before the Libyan conflict, French officials and nongovernmental experts were concerned about the political will of many fellow Europeans to join in military missions that might fall short of collective defense but are nonetheless important to French national interests. Libya, however, confirmed France's need to take a hard look at its current and potential future defense partnerships in Europe. And in some cases, the post-Libya fallout is already apparent.

Doubts About Germany

Since the early 1950s, French and German governments across the political spectrum have put the advancement of their bilateral relations—in economic, political and, since the 1980s, defense affairs—near or at the top of their international priorities. In turn, the Franco-German "locomotive" within the European Union frequently has led—or pushed—fellow Europeans to accept expanded integration and cooperation, including the development of CSDP. Over the past 2 years, Paris and Berlin have worked especially closely together (despite some underlying policy differences) to contain the sovereign debt crisis threatening the Eurozone. Indeed, French politicians and commentators by and large acknowledge Germany's leadership role in Europe regarding financial and economic matters, although they disagree strongly over whether the "German model" should be applied in France.

In important defense-related areas, however, French doubts about German policies and perspectives apparently have increased in recent years. For example, top officials reportedly were furious at Germany's abstention on UN Security Council Resolution 1973 and subsequent decision to withdraw German crew members from NATO Airborne Warning and Control System aircraft assigned to Operation *Unified Protector*. From Paris's viewpoint, these actions reflected, at best, Berlin's lack of appreciation for Europe's strategic stake in North Africa and, at worst, a strong and growing "anti-interventionist" strain in the German body politic.

French officials are reluctant to comment openly on their differences with Germany, given the overriding importance of the bilateral relationship in other areas. However, a range of government insiders and influential nongovernmental experts privately emphasize three areas of concern:

- For many in French military circles, Germany simply is not a partner of choice in operations involving combat risks. The "caveats" imposed by the Bundestag and German government on their military's operations in ISAF and as part of EU operations in Africa especially have rankled French officers; then–French Chief of Defense General Jean-Louis Georgelin referred to caveats as "poison for international coalitions" in a 2008 speech.[29] In addition, some French experts criticize the influence of German military unions, which they believe has impeded effective bilateral training and further tied the hands of German commanders in operational theaters. While few challenge the symbolic importance of the French-German brigade, an initiative launched in 1987 to intensify bilateral military cooperation, many dismiss the brigade's operational usefulness beyond limited peacekeeping tasks in a permissive environment.

- In recent years, divergent German and French views on nuclear weapon–related issues have become more evident. For example, according to well-informed French experts, Berlin—pushed in particular by Foreign Minister Guido Westerwelle—has sought language in NATO documents that, from Paris's perspective, would diminish the role of nuclear deterrence in Alliance strategy, advocate NATO's adoption of "negative security assurances," encourage the early withdrawal of U.S. nonstrategic nuclear weapons from Europe, and possibly put pressure on France to join future multilateral nuclear arms negotiations.[30] A broad consensus within the French strategic community opposes such moves, fearing they eventually would put significant pressure on France to change its nuclear doctrine and reduce its independent nuclear forces below the levels needed for credible deterrence.

■ Cooperation with Germany in the defense industrial arena has disappointed many in French government circles. Where instances of such cooperation have taken place—for example, in the development and production, along with other European partners, of the Airbus A400M transport aircraft, Tiger attack helicopter, and NH-90 transport helicopter—the programs apparently have encountered significant challenges in harmonizing requirements, controlling costs, and allocating work shares.[31] Germany's reluctance to partner on the MUSIS electro-optical satellite program has been a financial setback for the French, and the Eurofighter Typhoon multirole combat aircraft (a product of German defense industrial collaboration with British, Spanish, and Italian partners) directly competes with France's Rafale in third-party markets such as India.[32] Moreover, Paris reportedly was miffed by Berlin's cool reaction to its démarche in early 2011 when a high-level French delegation sought to reinvigorate defense cooperation with Germany along the lines of the November 2010 French-UK accords discussed below.

While French officials and nongovernmental experts broadly agree on the nature of their concerns regarding Germany as a partner in defense matters, they differ on how seriously these will affect the overall relationship between the two countries. For some respected retired French officers, Germany's accumulated experience in out-of-area operations since the early 1990s already has begun to transform German "military culture" and wean its political class from its heavy focus on territorial defense. In their view, once Germany's ongoing defense restructuring efforts and professionalization of the military are further advanced, the bilateral "locomotive" seen in economic, financial, and political affairs will extend to the defense sector as well.

Other French experts, inside and outside government, are decidedly pessimistic. They foresee a continuing trend, particularly among younger Germans, toward "pacifist" and "anti-nuclear" sentiments. Some see a large and growing disconnect between French security priorities in the Mediterranean region and, as one French interlocutor put it, Germany's "preoccupation with Mittel Europa."[33] For these experts, this France must look elsewhere for its strongest partnerships on in the defense area, while compartmentalizing its divergences with Germany to avoid harming the overall relationship.

CSDP in "Hibernation"

The EU goal, according to the White Book, should be to have the capability to "simultaneously conduct, over an extended period, two to three peacekeeping or peace enforcement operations and several smaller civilian missions in different theaters."[34] Building on this ambitious objective and the institutional changes agreed to in the EU Lisbon Treaty (which entered into force in December 2009), the Sarkozy government hoped to convince its EU partners to significantly expand their defense cooperation, especially in three areas: new deployable capabilities (such as strategic air transport, aerial refueling, multinational aircraft carrier task groups), improved intelligence-sharing and space-based surveillance systems, and establishing a permanent EU operational headquarters to plan and command its "autonomous" military and civilian missions.[35]

Nearly 4 years later, disappointment (if not disaffection) with CSDP appears widespread among French officials and nongovernmental experts. Their critiques fall into three broad categories.

Weak Appetite for Operations. In preparing the White Book, many French defense experts held that expanding the range, complexity, and number of EU military missions would be critical to building the domestic political support (in France and elsewhere in the European Union) for increased investment in capabilities. Since then, however, the EU appetite for new operational commitments has declined noticeably. France, to be sure, has been part of this trend; for example, top officials reportedly were upset that the 2008–2009 EU operation in Chad and the Central African Republic, which involved some 3,700 troops at its peak, proved more difficult and expensive, and required a much greater French commitment than Paris had anticipated. While several other EU military and civilian missions have been launched since 2008, most have been relatively modest in size, of limited duration, and low risk.

Slow Advance in Capabilities. The EU record in improving European military capabilities has been mixed at best. Since 2008, the EDA has tried to play a more active role in facilitating bilateral and regional cooperation among EU member states. Still, many of the problems identified by former EDA Director Nick Witney in 2008—for example, outsize investments in maintaining tanks, combat aircraft, and largely nondeployable land forces, while transport aircraft, helicopters, and intelligence, surveillance, and reconnaissance assets remain in chronically short supply—still plague the European Union today.[36] Defense spending by EU member states continues, with few exceptions, to drop. According to EDA data, in 2010, EU member states spent a total of €194 billion on defense, or 1.6 percent of their cumulative GDP. (If inflation is taken into account, this means that defense spending in real terms has declined since 2006.) Less than one-quarter of that total was spent on defense investment, with a relatively small (and decreasing) share going to research and technology. And despite EDA efforts to rationalize defense spending, only one-quarter of all procurement spending in the European Union during 2010 went to collaborative projects involving more than one member state.[37]

Structures Questioned. Meanwhile, one of the much touted innovations of the EU Lisbon Treaty—"Permanent Structured Cooperation" arrangements to encourage cooperation among members "whose military capabilities fulfill higher criteria and which have made more binding commitments to one another in this area with a view to the most demanding missions"— has not been implemented.[38] And the French-backed proposal to establish an EU operational headquarters remains blocked by the British, who view the idea as an unnecessary and costly duplication of NATO structures.

EU difficulties in coming to grips with the Libyan crisis in 2011 should not have surprised anyone. EU member states such as Germany that were reluctant to contribute to NATO's operation carried the same reservations into EU deliberations. Although some officials dispute the point, the European Union in effect turned down an early suggestion that it take charge of the maritime embargo component of the operation.[39] The European Union subsequently agreed to mount a CSDP military mission to facilitate humanitarian assistance to Libyan civilians, but its execution was made contingent upon a request from a UN agency widely believed to oppose any such military involvement. (In fact, the mission never advanced beyond the planning stage.)

EU *"immobilisme,"* as one French expert put it, sparked unaccustomed criticism from some of CSDP's strongest backers in Paris. The influential French daily *Le Monde* marked the launch of Operation *Unified Protector* by noting that "the EU failed miserably [in Libya]. . . . It was incapable of agreeing on what action to take, how to deal with the Libyan opposition, and the legitimacy of the use of force."[40] Looking back at EU performance in Libya, Guillaud told French senators in October 2011: "I'm used to saying that [European defense] is hibernating. This is an optimistic view, because it implies that there will be an awakening, a springtime. European defense missed the boat in Libya."[41]

No French government will abandon CSDP. Despite setbacks and lowered expectations, CSDP will remain, as the above mentioned interministerial study suggests, an indispensable element of longstanding French strategy to promote the European Union as a global actor in defense and security affairs. Still, a subtle but potentially important shift in French thinking appears to be gaining traction. During the past decade, many French officials and experts equated the term *European defense* with CSDP (or European Security and Defense Policy [ESDP], as it was known before the Lisbon Treaty). Increasingly, however, many use the term to describe (or justify) a more diverse set of intertwined French relationships—within NATO, EU, and various other multilateral and bilateral frameworks. The twin strategic goals of such relationships have not changed: to bolster the defense capabilities and, eventually, the political will of European partners to join with France in its activist approach toward promoting "European interests." While some in France's strategic affairs community might bridle at any perceived downgrading of the EU institutional role, others suggest that the shift in thinking simply reflects a more pragmatic approach to constructing a viable European defense.

French-British Defense Cooperation: A New Route to European Defense?

France's new interest in pragmatic solutions explains its growing defense ties with the United Kingdom, the European country that comes closest to sharing France's sense of bearing global responsibilities. At their Lancaster House summit in November 2010, Sarkozy and Prime Minister David Cameron announced a new and ambitious blueprint for their relationship consisting of three parts: a declaration of broad goals and principles, a treaty that establishes a framework for specific cooperation in nonnuclear areas, and a treaty on cooperation in nuclear-related matters. And following their meeting in Paris in February 2012, the two leaders pledged additional efforts.[42]

Strategic Context for French-British Cooperation

To be sure, declarations of intent to strengthen French-British cooperation are not a recent development. In February 2003, for example, French President Jacques Chirac and Prime Minister Tony Blair declared that they "cannot imagine a situation in which the vital interests of one of our two countries . . . could be threatened without the vital interests of the other also being threatened."[43] They agreed to expand cooperation between their national planning and operations staffs "to enhance their interoperability to prepare for contingencies where they may be called to act together at very short notice." They also agreed to develop the interoperability of their aircraft carrier groups and industrial cooperation on their respective carrier procurement programs. Yet, within several weeks of their summit, Paris and London were deeply divided over the invasion of Iraq, which at one point involved approximately one-fifth of the entire British armed forces. And in 2008, cooperation on aircraft carrier procurement, which already had been plagued by divergent design requirements and work-share issues, was effectively shelved when the French dropped plans to build their second carrier.

In the past few years, however, several factors have improved the prospects for meaningful and sustained French-British defense cooperation. Despite past recriminations over Iraq,

French and British policymakers and analysts have come to share similar assessments of the international security environment, especially regarding weapons and ballistic missile proliferation, terrorism, and threats to free access in the global commons (cyber, maritime, and space). The two countries have many overlapping interests in the Persian Gulf, Southwest Asia, sub-Saharan Africa, and Balkans.

Regarding capabilities, French and British armed forces are similar in many respects, although French land forces are about 15 percent larger. Both countries have—and want to maintain—"full spectrum" military capabilities, including nuclear and conventional components. According to their respective security strategies, both want to be able to deploy and sustain—alone, if necessary—highly capable "intervention" forces of approximately 30,000 personnel, with aviation and maritime support.[44] Although the overall British defense budget is somewhat larger (due in part to higher personnel expenditures), their investment and research levels are fairly close. Together, the two countries account for nearly half of Europe's total defense spending and about two-thirds of its research and development effort.

When it comes to operations, French and British officials frequently point out that their militaries share an expeditionary mindset. Over the past two decades, both countries have been among the top contributors, including in combat roles, to NATO-led operations in the Balkans, Afghanistan, and Libya. Both have participated in various (and concurrent) national, EU-led, and UN-led operations, although the French engagement in operations outside NATO—especially in Africa and Lebanon—has been significantly larger.

In addition, changes in the surrounding international context have given new impetus to French-British defense cooperation. According to senior French and British officials, the French decision to rejoin NATO military structures fully has been a critical element in their rapprochement in defense matters. Beyond its political significance, the presence of senior French officers within those structures has expanded day-to-day contact between the two militaries on interoperability, doctrine, operational planning, and training issues.

At the same time, France's lowered expectations for CSDP—in practice, if not always in rhetoric—has eased longstanding British concerns (especially within Conservative Party ranks) that the French vision for European defense necessarily would favor EU structures to the detriment of NATO. Indeed, London and Paris apparently have reached a tacit understanding to "agree to disagree" on politically charged aspects of CSDP. For example, while the British oppose the permanent EU operational headquarters advocated by the French and other EU member states, London has not blocked low-key arrangements to enhance the role of Brussels-based EU military staffs coordinating operations in the Horn of Africa region.

Moreover, the French and British no longer view cooperation as an option to improve capabilities; rather, it is seen as necessary for both countries to preserve their already constrained ability to act, either independently or with others, as global powers. As one respected French expert has explained, "Defense capabilities, both the 'legacy' systems inherited from the Cold War and the emerging requirements, have proved more expensive with each new generation of equipment. . . . The negative trends of economic austerity, defense inflation, and a demanding strategic environment are rapidly converging into a downward spiral that, if nothing is done, will prove the end of the defense game for the two middle powers of Europe."[45]

Finally, U.S. willingness during the Libyan crisis to share the political and military leadership spotlight with France and the United Kingdom surprised Paris and had a ricochet effect on French-British cooperation. It raised questions in the minds of some French officials regarding Washington's readiness to play a prominent role in future contingencies in and near Europe that are deemed not to pose a direct threat to American interests. "To avoid similar surprises in the future," one eminent nongovernmental expert advised, "European allies will need to acquire some weapons which the United States alone in NATO currently possesses. France and the United Kingdom . . . should lead the way."[46] Some French analysts see an additional factor at play: the British political class, they suggest, has been "disillusioned" with American leadership in Iraq and Afghanistan, making cooperation with France more appealing.[47]

Areas for Cooperation and Possible Constraints

The centerpiece of the Lancaster House treaty on nuclear matters is an agreement to construct by 2014 a new joint hydrodynamic-radiographic facility in France and a new joint technology development center in the United Kingdom. Together, these facilities will enable each country to carry out experiments in a secure environment necessary to ensure the safety, reliability, and performance of their respective nuclear weapons stockpile without nuclear explosive testing. (France and the United Kingdom have ratified the Comprehensive Test Ban Treaty, which prohibits such explosive testing.) As the treaty makes clear—and as senior French and British officials have emphasized to their respective parliaments—joint use of the facilities does not imply that the parties will share all data gained from the experiments. Indeed, both the design of the facilities and conduct of the actual experiments will reflect the parties' insistence on protecting sensitive details of their independent national deterrents. A senior British defense official stated in March 2011 that the treaty "does not involve the sharing of any nuclear deterrent capability, such as submarine patrols."[48] Despite such constraints, however, this unprecedented level of cooperation enjoys broad political support in Paris and London. Moreover, its anticipated cost advantages appear to be substantial;

one study estimates that each country will save some €450 million in infrastructure costs associated with the two facilities over the next decade or so.[49]

In parallel with their nuclear cooperation, the French and British are working together to improve their conventional capabilities across a range of missions, including possible "high-intensity" warfare. They are developing a Combined Joint Expeditionary Force comprised of brigade-level land components, as well as maritime and air components with associated headquarters and support units. Although not a standing force, it will be available on relatively short notice for operations under bilateral, NATO, EU, or UN auspices, or as members of a "coalition of the willing." According to French military experts, the command and control structures for the new combined force will be in place in 2012; following a 5-year exercise program, the force will reach full operational capability in 2016. Meanwhile, the French and British will work toward having the ability to deploy an integrated aircraft carrier strike group by the early 2020s, with British combat aircraft capable of operating from a French carrier and vice versa.

On the defense industrial front, French and British plans for cooperation on military systems development have been heavily influenced by their experience in Afghanistan, Libya, and—for the British—Iraq. Unmanned aerial systems (armed and unarmed drones) are among their top priorities; a "Joint Program Office" created in 2011 is working with BAE Systems (on the British side) and Dassault Aviation (for the French) to assess both intermediate and more advanced technologies. Efforts are under way as well to cooperate in areas such as training and support for the A400M military transport aircraft, which both militaries will begin to receive in the next few years; submarine technologies, including sonar equipment; maritime mine and improvised explosive device countermeasures; satellite communications; and precision-guided munitions.

Still, while French officials and nongovernmental experts broadly agree on the rationale for, and positive trajectory of, the French-British rapprochement on defense, their assessments of its likely pace differ. For some, it remains largely a top-down initiative that risks being slowed when political leaders in Paris and London either turn their attention elsewhere—as they did in late 2011 and early 2012, when Sarkozy and Cameron sharply criticized each other on EU financial regulatory policies—or find themselves on different sides of an important strategic issue, as happened with Iraq in 2003.

The latter possibility evidently concerns some British politicians as well. Hence, during the House of Commons debate on ratification of the two Lancaster House treaties, the Labour Party's "shadow defense secretary" insisted on "an absolute guarantee that [the treaties] do not place any limitation whatever on the United Kingdom's ability to act independently in all circumstances in the protection of our unique interests across the world, including the defense of our overseas territories and in respect of the deployment of our armed forces or our military assets."[50] In response, then–Defense Secretary Liam Fox confirmed that the treaties place no limitation on either country's ability to deploy forces "when [it] believes that it is in its national interest to do so."[51]

Others worry about perceived hesitations among the respective military services. Interoperability and cooperation between the French air force and Royal Air Force are quite good, but the land forces (including special forces) have had much less experience working together, even in Afghanistan. Navy-to-navy relations apparently fall somewhere in between, with good operational cooperation in the Persian Gulf region and Horn of Africa, but with certain historical grievances (Mers-el-Kebir on the French side, the Falklands war on the British) apparently not entirely forgotten.[52] French and British officers express a range of views on the degree and impact of perceived differences between their respective military cultures. But the planned expansion of joint facilities, headquarters staffs, response forces, training, and professional military exchanges likely will narrow those differences over time.

A more likely challenge to French-British cooperation will be to sort out the defense industrial relationships necessary to meet their agreed objectives regarding equipment and capabilities. In this area, the two countries' record to date is mixed. Some success stories exist: the Storm Shadow/Scalp air-launched cruise missile, which performed well in the Libyan conflict, was a product of MBDA, a multinational group formed in 2001 (after the merger of leading French, British, and Italian missile producers) that now represents approximately 70 percent of the European missile industry.[53] Building on this, the French and British authorities will work with MBDA on possible advanced cruise missiles and antiship weapons.

In other areas, however, such as advanced combat aircraft and some armored systems, French and British companies compete for third-party sales. Moreover, some French defense experts are skeptical that the planned bilateral cooperation on unmanned aerial systems and naval construction will proceed smoothly, given the nature of the industrial groups involved and pressures in both countries to protect domestic jobs. Also, organizational differences between French and British government agencies charged with defense research, development, and procurement apparently exacerbate their difficulties in aligning their respective defense industry partners.[54] In the case of particularly complex and expensive projects, such as development and production of fifth generation combat aircraft or new attack and ballistic missile submarines, many French experts expect the British to look first and foremost to the United States.[55]

Impact of French Elections

Defense issues traditionally have not been at the forefront of French presidential election campaigns. This year's race, which is dominated by economic, employment, and societal issues (such as immigration policy), is no exception.[56]

On many strategic issues, the two candidates most likely to face each other in the May 6 runoff, Sarkozy and Hollande, appear to have similar positions. For example, in Hollande's March 2012 speech on defense, his description of major threats to French security—including terrorism, proliferation, instability in the Mediterranean region, and Iranian nuclear developments—echo many of the principal conclusions of the White Book and 2012 interministerial study.[57] He reaffirmed the importance of maintaining the nuclear deterrent as a necessary "life insurance" to defend French "vital interests," and specifically pledged to keep France's air-delivered and ballistic missile submarine components. Moreover, several of his declared priorities—for example, improving intelligence and space capabilities, meeting operational needs for deployed forces, and strengthening France's defense industrial base while increasing cooperation with its European partners, especially the United Kingdom—track closely with the current government's policies.

However, Hollande charged in his speech that Sarkozy's decision to rejoin NATO military structures was "precipitous" and that several years later, "France has not gained any significant benefit." Hollande promised to "evaluate" the decision, weighing the advantages of participation in the military structures, its relationship to European defense, and its implications for French "independence." At the same time, he did not state any intention, if elected, to withdraw from those structures.

As the campaign intensifies, Sarkozy and Hollande likely will inject defense issues to their list of disagreements over economic and social issues. Sarkozy supporters already have suggested that his challenger is ill-prepared to assume the president's commander-in-chief responsibilities, since he has not served in any governmental capacity beyond his position as a member of parliament. Sarkozy might point to Hollande's opposition in 2009 to the decision to rejoin NATO military structures as evidence of an alleged "ideological" bias against NATO and, more generally, a lack of familiarity with political-military affairs. For his part, Hollande likely will sharpen his critique of Sarkozy's alleged failure to reinvigorate CSDP in parallel with the rapprochement with NATO, even though some Hollande advisors privately acknowledge that a lack of political will by other EU members, not French policy, has been the major stumbling block.

Afghanistan might be another point of contention. Following the murder of four French soldiers by an Afghan soldier in January 2012, Sarkozy announced his intention to withdraw all French "combat" troops by the end of 2013, while leaving behind "a few hundred" military trainers to work with the Afghan national security forces.[58] In his March speech, Hollande promised to accomplish the withdrawal of "combat" forces by the end of 2012, although he added an ambiguous reference (not unlike Sarkozy's) indicating that France would seek to coordinate closely with its NATO Allies. However, Hollande was silent on the question of possible future French military participation in training Afghan forces.

Implications for the NATO Summit

Sarkozy or, if elected, Hollande would not come to Chicago with the intention of acting as a spoiler. Each would want to highlight France's prominent role in the Libyan conflict as a positive example of European willingness to share global responsibilities with the United States. And each would vigorously defend France's established "red lines" regarding Alliance nuclear weapons policy; hence, any perceived interference with French nuclear doctrine or implied tradeoff between nuclear deterrence and missile defense would be rejected. Still, Sarkozy and Hollande might differ in other respects.

If Sarkozy were reelected, he might come to Chicago determined to play a more central and high-profile role than was the case at the November 2010 Lisbon Summit. Afghanistan likely would be at or near the top of his concerns. French opinion polls indicate strong opposition to continued French military involvement there, and even with Sarkozy's mandate renewed, his center-right party likely will face an uphill battle to keep its majority in the National Assembly (the lower house of the French parliament) in elections scheduled for June 10 and 17.[59] These domestic political considerations, combined with growing impatience with the Afghan situation within government and military circles, would make it difficult for Sarkozy to back away from his 2013 target date.

Smart defense—NATO's concept for developing, acquiring, and maintaining military capabilities through increased multinational cooperation—might be another contentious issue. Influential French governmental officials and defense industry leaders reportedly suspect Washington of promoting a "buy American" agenda under the guise of "smart defense," especially in programs involving the NATO Alliance Ground Surveillance system, European participation in NATO missile defense, and the proposed creation of a "pooling and sharing" arrangement for tanker aircraft. During his campaign, Sarkozy has adopted increasingly protectionist rhetoric; in March, for example, he proposed EU legislation requiring member states to favor procurement of European-made products. Hence, he would be likely to resist any smart defense package that does not provide tangible opportunities for the French defense industry.

Hollande, if elected, likely would come to Chicago with somewhat different priorities. Establishing a good working relationship with President Barack Obama would be a central goal for the new French leader. But Hollande would face the difficult task of reassuring the American and other allied leaders of French solidarity and broad policy continuity, while simultaneously appearing to honor his campaign promises only weeks before the National Assembly elections.

The timing of the summit poses special problems for Hollande. If victorious on May 6, he likely will be inaugurated on May 16. During that interim, he will be preoccupied with many pressing tasks, such as deciding ministerial and other high-level appointments. This will leave him little time to prepare for the May 18–19 G-8 meeting at Camp David and, shortly thereafter, the NATO summit.

According to French experts, Hollande's senior advisors on defense matters have established an informal network of contacts with a small number of high-ranking career civil servants and diplomats in the defense and foreign affairs ministries. This network apparently has helped Hollande and his team to keep abreast of government policies in key defense areas. It is not clear, however, whether such informal channels are used to share the details of various issues and texts now under discussion at NATO for approval at Chicago.

Hence, if Hollande is elected, negotiations with French officials on final summit documents might be complicated by their need to gain approval from, or introduce changes demanded by, newly installed ministers and presidential staff. On Afghanistan, for example, Hollande's stated timetable for withdrawing French troops might be harder for the United States and other Allies to accommodate than Sarkozy's. Regarding NATO missile defense, some Hollande advisors caution that he would be more reserved than Sarkozy regarding possible French contributions to the NATO missile defense program. Prominent Socialist Party figures reportedly have deep concerns over its cost, efficacy, and future command and control arrangements, while others fear it could undermine the credibility of the French nuclear deterrent.

On the other hand, Hollande advisors appear confident that he would reassure allied leaders in Chicago that France will not withdraw from NATO military structures following his promised "evaluation" of the benefits of participation. "We are keeping our place [in the military structures]," according to Jean-Yves Le Drian, Hollande's closest confidant on defense. "We would not have done [the reintegration], but we are not going to undo everything."[60] Indeed, according to one advisor, Hollande would insist on keeping French officers in top-level NATO positions—in particular, as the Supreme Commander, ACT. Moreover, in view of the French air force's role in the Libyan conflict, Hollande (like Sarkozy) would nominate French officers for top-level positions in NATO's new air component commands.

Defense Spending Reductions Foreseen

According to a variety of French defense experts, further defense budget cuts are inevitable regardless of the results of the presidential and National Assembly elections. If Sarkozy is re-elected, he is widely expected to introduce tough new austerity measures to bring France in line with the tighter EU fiscal rules that he played a key role (along with German Chancellor Angela Merkel) in achieving. Given the added pressure this will put on so-called social budgets (such as education, health care, and public sector pensions), few believe that Sarkozy could afford politically to spare defense spending.

Many experts believe that Sarkozy would want to protect, first and foremost, spending for the nuclear deterrent, which represents roughly 20 percent of the defense investment budget. In a declining defense budget, this would squeeze the resources available for maintaining or modernizing conventional systems. According to some experts, French armored forces and older aircraft would be among the top candidates for cutbacks, since less painful measures—for example, the sale of excess military properties and state-controlled radio frequencies—apparently already have been exhausted. While the withdrawal of most French troops from Afghanistan would produce savings in the long run, the near-term costs of repatriating equipment that cannot be left behind could be substantial.

Unlike Sarkozy, Hollande publicly has hinted at future defense cuts, noting that "there are savings to be made," although he has not offered specific examples.[61] He has pledged to keep overall defense spending constant relative to total public sector spending; hence, in principle, defense (which now represents around 3.3 percent of that total) would not suffer disproportionately if deficit cutting measures were necessary. Moreover, according to one defense advisor, Hollande's pursuit of growth-oriented policies (combined with much higher taxes on the wealthy) would ease pressure on all government spending, including the defense budget. However, if those policies were to fail and a new round of austerity were unavoidable, there is little doubt that Hollande's government would be more inclined than Sarkozy's to protect social budgets important to the French Left.

The United States and *"la Grande Nation"*

Since 2008, U.S.-French relations have grown closer in a number of defense-related areas. They have been helped by a broad albeit imperfect convergence on many key strategic issues, such as the threats posed by the proliferation of weapons of mass destruction and their delivery means (in particular, by Iranian nuclear and ballistic missile programs); weakened but still determined terrorist networks; state and nonstate actors able to exploit vulnerabilities in the global commons; and the possibility, even if remote, of a major military confrontation in or near Europe or the Asia-Pacific region. Thanks to France's return to NATO military structures and its growing defense cooperation with the United Kingdom, Washington and Paris should be better positioned to address one of their most serious mutual concerns: Europe's shortfalls in key military capabilities and, in some cases, its lack of political will to use military force. To do so, U.S. and French officials might consider some new approaches to working together bilaterally and with others.

Deepening Military-to-Military Relations

By nearly all accounts, the U.S. and French militaries enjoy excellent relations at their most senior levels. These are maintained by periodic consultations and counterpart visits involving top officers of the U.S. Joint Staff, French Defense Staff, and the U.S. and French military services. Moreover, cooperation between the two militaries in operations over the past decade—including but not limited to Afghanistan, Libya, and maritime security missions in the Persian Gulf, Mediterranean, and Horn of Africa regions—often has been exceptionally close.

A number of other arrangements help to sustain U.S.-French military-to-military relations. Many American and French officers and NCOs work together in various NATO command and staff structures. A total of a few dozen French and American officers serve as "exchange" officers in tactical units; such arrangements might involve, for example, a U.S. Air Force pilot assigned to a Mirage 2000 squadron in France and a French air force pilot flying with an A-10 squadron in the United States. Smaller numbers of French and American officers take up to 1-year courses at each others' professional military education institutions. And a handful of officers on each side serve as "liaison" officers between planning staffs (for example, a French officer works at U.S. Central Command headquarters in the Coalition Planning Group) or between counterpart organizations (an American officer in France facilitates exchanges between the training and doctrine commands of the two armies).

However, the U.S. and French militaries have been slow to establish arrangements to embed senior officers at strategic levels in their respective military structures, where they could work side by side with their host country colleagues and, for the most part, within the host's chain of command. The U.S. and French air forces each have one senior officer in the other's strategic studies group, but this appears to be a unique arrangement for the two countries. The

U.S. military has a significantly more developed set of embedded arrangements with traditionally close English-speaking allies, as do the French with their closest European partners.

A gradually expanded and more structured program of embedding senior American and French officers at strategic levels in a small number of national staffs and headquarters could bring substantial benefits to both countries, including cross-fertilization of their planning and operational expertise at influential nodes where military strategies, policies, and requirements are formulated; ability to exchange information quickly at senior working levels; better appreciation for their respective problem-solving cultures; and building networks for future cooperation. Enhancing intellectual interoperability between American and French officers upstream in their national defense structures would facilitate practical cooperation between the two militaries downstream—for example, in NATO commands in a range of ongoing field operations and in potential future contingencies. In addition, embedded officers also might serve as "shock absorbers," helping to maintain the critical element of trust between militaries when the two countries disagree over specific policies or tactics. Indeed, American and French officers who have participated in such arrangements testify to benefits in many of these areas.

Before establishing such a program, Washington and Paris would need to take an in-depth look at reciprocity and, in particular, information-sharing issues. Neither military expects unrestricted access to the other's classified data networks, but both have an interest in removing any unnecessary impediments to bilateral and, potentially, trilateral cooperation with the United Kingdom. Given the evolving U.S. military footprint in Europe and the likelihood of U.S.-French cooperation in a range of future contingencies, an effective embed program might prove to be a relatively low cost, high return investment.

Defense Industry Issues

While the United States and France cooperate closely on many strategic and operational issues, their interactions on defense industrial matters often have been strained and, at times, confrontational. Contributing factors include direct competition between U.S. and French industrial concerns (particularly in the aerospace industry) for sales to third parties and, in some cases, to each other's military; related disputes over the extent of government subsidies provided to those industrial concerns; and differences over arms export policies and practices, especially where technology transfer issues are involved.

Moreover, where controversies arise, they can be exacerbated by the mismatch of interests. As seen from Paris, the U.S. defense industry casts a huge shadow over the potential market for French products, with all that that implies for their domestic employment and, in some cases, the price of armaments for the French military. With some notable exceptions, competition with French firms (or European consortiums with important French participation) captures less national-level attention in the United States.[62]

The growing multinational (including transatlantic) connections of some defense companies, combined with Washington's steps in recent years to streamline U.S. export and technology transfer controls, have mitigated these concerns somewhat. But they are still pervasive, at least on the French side, as suggested by the aforementioned French perceptions regarding U.S. motivations and smart defense. This, in turn, creates an unhealthy atmosphere for U.S.-French and, more broadly, U.S.-European cooperation to improve defense capabilities in what promises to be an extended period of relatively austere defense budgets.

Given this situation, Washington and Paris might usefully consider how to improve their dialogue and reduce the risk of misperceptions regarding defense industrial questions. A number of bilateral government-to-government agreements already exist for joint work in specific program areas—for example, military communications, maritime surveillance, and chemical, biological, radiological, and nuclear detection and protection. Some of these have received high-level attention, such as the bilateral statement on principles for space situational awareness signed by then–Secretary of Defense Robert Gates and then–Defense Minister Alain Juppé in February 2011. And American and French defense and military officials share an interest in expanded exchanges on cyber security.

Government-to-government relationships in such areas might be enhanced by the creation of a U.S.-France High Level Working Group, similar to the body commissioned pursuant to the Lancaster House Treaty on Defense and Security Cooperation.[63] Senior U.S. and French defense officials could use such a forum to clarify their respective research, development, and acquisition strategies and provide better overall guidance for industrial and armament cooperation, bringing in, where appropriate, representatives of French and U.S. industries.

Trilateral Cooperation

The deepening British-French defense relationship is fully consistent with key U.S. strategic priorities, including the promotion of enhanced capacity, interoperability, and political will among American allies and partners to share the costs and responsibilities of global leadership. As demonstrated during the 2011 Libyan crisis, once Washington, London, and Paris agree on their strategic goals, their militaries need to be capable of acting effectively and on short notice, either as a "coalition of the willing" or within a NATO framework. All three will want to preserve that capability, even as the United States proceeds to "rebalance toward the Asia-Pacific region."[64]

Moreover, given the certainty of continuing tight constraints on defense spending (if not further reductions) on both sides of the Atlantic, trilateral cooperation will become more important to preserve core capabilities and competencies within the Alliance as a whole. This would be especially true if, as some European experts predict, the "Afghanistan effect" were to make many Allies even more disinclined to involve themselves in expeditionary operations.

Fortunately, a solid foundation for U.S.-British-French military cooperation already exists. The three air forces are probably the most advanced in this regard, thanks to a now decades-long history of partnering in operations within and outside NATO, well-developed officer exchanges in tactical units, and regular strategic-level consultations and exercises.[65] Structured cooperation among the three navies and land forces reportedly is less frequent, but there are good reasons to expand those relationships. For example, the three navies have cooperated closely in the Persian Gulf region, and an Iranian threat to freedom of navigation through the Strait of Hormuz would make such cooperation even more important. In the Horn of Africa and West African regions, the three countries share a common interest in training African security forces in counterterrorism and peacekeeping skills—a mission that largely falls to American, British, and French army personnel, including special forces. Improved coordination of their respective efforts and possibly greater role specialization should be explored. Models for coordination already exist, including the "P3 +" effort in West Africa in which the United States, United Kingdom, and France have divided up responsibility for supporting the strategic, operational, and tactical levels of training of national elements for the standby force of the Economic Community of West African States.

Once considered a strict taboo, the British-French cooperation on technologies associated with nuclear stockpile stewardship was a subject of U.S.-British consultations before and after the Lancaster House treaty, according to Fox's November 2010 statement to the House of Commons.[66] Both Washington and London apparently were particularly intent on avoiding any breach of their mutual obligations under the 1958 Mutual Defense Treaty, which covers, inter alia, cooperation on nuclear weapons design, development, and maintenance. Noting that France also cooperates "very closely" with the United States on nuclear weapons issues, Fox acknowledged that "there has been discussion for some time about whether the [nuclear] relationship should be trilateral, given the cost of the programmes, but the decision has been taken that for the moment, the double bilateral relationship will continue."[67]

In principle, a U.S.-British-French trilateral relationship could take many forms, including but not limited to intensified information-sharing on the nuclear capabilities of states outside the trilateral group, high-level political-military discussions of nuclear targeting and employment doctrine, shared access to submarine maintenance facilities, and coordination of ballistic missile submarine deployment schedules and/or areas. However, as a recent study correctly notes, "Cooperation between the three would be an intriguing response to an uncertain strategic environment, in a political climate in which the role of nuclear weapons is once more a matter for debate . . . [but] one can imagine any number of political, legal and technical obstacles, as well perhaps as a British reluctance to make the transatlantic relationship less 'special.'"[68]

French authorities also will tread carefully where nuclear matters are concerned. A broad and deep consensus exists in the French political class, defense establishment, and strategic affairs community on core tenets of nuclear policy: the credibility of the French deterrent rests on the president's ability to decide "independently" whether and how to use it in defense of the nation's "vital interests"; France will maintain the minimal level of nuclear forces consistent with its security needs, but its force level will not depend on that of other nuclear powers; and a credible deterrent can only be assured if France maintains, on a national basis, the specialized technological and industrial competencies necessary to build and maintain its nuclear forces.

Finding a path to advance France's bilateral or, eventually, trilateral nuclear cooperation with the United Kingdom and the United States without putting into question one or more of these core tenets will not be easy. According to some French experts, however, there might not be a pressing need to make any quick decisions on this score. In their analysis, thanks to the extensive modernization programs executed over the past decade, the government has another 7 to 10 years to decide on its next round of major force recapitalization efforts. This would give the French time to consider whether and, if so, how to link their forces more closely to those of the British.

Still, this leaves open the possibility of a French initiative in the nuclear policy area, which some experts hope will be considered in the post-election preparations of a new White Book. When France returned to NATO military structures in 2009, it did not join the Nuclear Planning Group and its subordinate bodies, where the 27 other defense ministers and their senior representatives meet at regular intervals to discuss a range of nuclear policy matters—from the safety, security, and survivability of nuclear weapons to wider issues such as nuclear arms control and nuclear proliferation.

But leading figures within the French strategic community are now suggesting that France reconsider its position and become a full participant in NATO nuclear policy discussions (perhaps under a renamed and reconfigured committee).[69] As one respected retired general who supports the idea recently asked in *Le Monde*:

In a world of globalized threats, how can one believe that our nuclear doctrine's notion of "vital interests" can be based solely on our national logic? How could we imagine using our nuclear weapons without earlier reference to our allies? It's not a question of losing our decision-making autonomy, but of sharing planning and targeting. The United States is a member [of the Nuclear Planning Group] without abandoning its national planning.[70]

As some French experts point out, the political benefits of such a move could be significant, since it would knit together France's larger role in NATO structures, aspirations for greater political and military cohesion among Europeans, and closer bilateral relationship with the United Kingdom and the United States—all without sacrificing its "independence."

A Cautionary Note

The French, at times, can be difficult partners for the United States and other Europeans in defense-related matters. Many of their attributes—among these are their sense of global responsibilities, pride in their national capabilities, and willingness to use force and accept risk, if necessary, in pursuit of their strategic interests—make them highly valued contributors to transatlantic security. But others—such as their tendency to cast France as the preeminent defender of "European interests" against allegedly excessive American influence—can try the patience of European and U.S. leaders alike.

Fortunately, French defense efforts in recent years have demonstrated the former attributes more often than the latter. If current trends hold, increased pragmatic cooperation with the United Kingdom—and, one hopes, other Europeans—can help France emerge from the current period of defense austerity with its most important capabilities relatively intact.

For the United States, more is at stake than the health of the French defense establishment. France's policies, capabilities, and operational commitments can play an important role in shaping those of many other Europeans. By working even more closely with its oldest ally, the United States can help ensure the credibility and effectiveness of the Alliance as a whole.

Notes

[1] Hearing of Admiral Édouard Guillaud, Assemblée nationale, Commission de la défense nationale et des forces armées, October 5, 2011.

[2] "The International and Strategic Evolutions Faced by France: Preparatory document for the update of the White paper on Defence and national security" (Interministerial study), Secrétariat général de la defense et de la sécurité nationale, March 12, 2012, available at <www.sgdsn.gouv.fr/IMG/pdf/Doc_preparatoire_LBDSN_UK-2012-V2_WEB_Protected.pdf>.

[3] For background on the 2008 *White Book on Defense and National* Security (White Book), see Leo G. Michel, *Defense Transformation* à la française *and U.S. Interests*, INSS Strategic Forum 233 (Washington, DC: NDU Press, 2008). See also *Défense et Sécurité nationale: le Livre Blanc* (White Book) (Paris: Odile Jacob/Documentation Française, June 2008).

[4] Interministerial study, 8.

[5] Ibid., 7–8.

[6] Ibid., 8, 50.

[7] Ibid., 48.

[8] Ibid., 51.

[9] International Monetary Fund World Economic Outlook, "Mild Slowdown of the Global Expansion, and Increasing Risks," June 17, 2011, available at <www.imf.org/external/pubs/ft/weo/2011/update/02/index.htm>.

[10] Department of Defense (DOD), *Sustaining U.S. Global Leadership: Priorities for 21st Century Defense* (Washington, DC: DOD, January 2012), available at <www.defense.gov/news/Defense_Strategic_Guidance.pdf>.

[11] Figures used are nominal (not adjusted for inflation). See "Annuaire statistique de la defense 2010/2011," Ministere de la defense, June 2011, available at <www.defense.gouv.fr/sga/le-sga-en-action/economie-et-statistiques/annuaire-statistique-de-la-defense#>.

[12] Ibid.

[13] Ibid.

[14] Ibid.

[15] French embassy figures as of November 2007, available at <www.ambafrance-us.org/spip.php?article514>.

[16] French Ministry of Defense figures for January 2012, available at <www.defense.gouv.fr/operations/rubriques_complementaires/carte-des-operations-exterieures>.

[17] Interministerial study, 53.

[18] Ibid.

[19] For example, former conservative Prime Minister Alain Juppé wrote op-eds expressing deep skepticism regarding rapprochement with the North Atlantic Treaty Organization (NATO) in 2008 and early 2009. He later became minister of defense and, in early 2011, was named minister of foreign affairs.

[20] Common Security and Defense Policy is described in the (Lisbon) Treaty on European Union, Title V, in particular Article 17, available at <www.consilium.europa.eu/uedocs/cmsUpload/Treaty%20on%20European%20Union%20-%20Title%20V.pdf>.

[21] Then–Foreign Minister Bernard Kouchner reportedly agreed with Nicholas Sarkozy's decision on NATO, but this apparently was not the case for some of his assistants.

[22] Interviews with author, September 2011 and March 2012.

[23] Hearing of Admiral Édouard Guillaud, Sénat, Commission de la défense nationale et des forces armées, October 12, 2011.

[24] Interviews with author, September 2011.

[25] See editorial by Director General for Armament Laurent Collet-Billon in *Bilan d'activités 2011 de la* DGA, available at <www.defense.gouv.fr/dga>.

[26] In interviews with the author, other French military experts have suggested that the army's helicopter pilots may have assumed unnecessary risks due to shortcomings in intraservice coordination with their air force and naval assets.

[27] Interviews with author, September 2011.

[28] United Nations S/RES/1973 (2011), Security Council Resolution 1973 (2011), Adopted by the Security Council at its 6498th meeting, on March 17, 2011, available at <www.un.org/News/Press/docs/2011/sc10200.doc.htm>.

[29] Interview of General Jean-Louis Georgelin, chief of defense, France, on Europe 1 Radio, September 22, 2008, available at <www.defense.gouv.fr/ema/le-chef-d-etat-major/interventions/interviews/22-09-08-interview-du-cema-sur-europe-1>. General Georgelin did not cite Germany by name, but it was clear from the context that he had Germany in mind—a point confirmed to the author by another French officer.

[30] A *negative security assurance* is a guarantee by a state that possesses nuclear weapons that it will not use or threaten to use nuclear weapons against states that do not possess nuclear weapons. The Obama administration's 2010 Nuclear Posture Review states that the United States "will not use or threaten to use nuclear weapons against non-nuclear weapons states that are party to the Nuclear Non-Proliferation Treaty and in compliance with their nuclear non-proliferation obligations." See *Nuclear Posture Review Report* (Washington, DC: DOD, April 2010), 15, available at <www.defense.gov/npr/docs/2010%20Nuclear%20Posture%20Review%20Report.pdf>.

[31] German officials apparently share many of these concerns. See remarks of German Minister of Defense Thomas de Maizière to French National Assembly's Commission on National Defense and Armed Forces, July 6, 2011, available at <www.assembleenationale.fr/13/cr-cdef/10-11/c1011046.asp#P2_68>.

[32] Arms sales can roil defense industrial relations in other ways. For example, according to one published report: "Franco-German relations could suffer from a huge arms deal. Paris obviously intends to supply two to four new stealth frigates to the Greek Navy. Since the country is highly in debt at the moment and unable to pay €300 million per vessel, Paris has offered the government in Athens to use the frigates free of charge for a period of five years. The ships, which were developed by the state-run DCNS shipyard, should only be paid after that with a discount of €100 million or be taken over by the French Navy. This deal does not go down well with the German competitors that have fought for the contract for years." *Der Spiegel Online*, October 17, 2011.

[33] Interviews with author, September 2011.

[34] White Book, 89.

[35] "Autonomous" European Union (EU) missions are those conducted without cooperation or support from NATO. Under the 2003 "Berlin Plus" arrangements, the EU can have access to certain collective assets and capabilities of NATO, including command arrangements and assistance in operational planning, for an EU-led operation.

[36] Nick Whitney, *Re-energising Europe's Security and Defence Policy* (London: European Council on Foreign Relations, July 2008), available at <http://ecfr.3cdn.net/c66a5b8b70f2e804a0_6xm6iywb0.pdf>.

[37] European Defence Agency, "Europe and the United States Defence Expenditure in 2010," January 12, 2012, available at <www.eda.europa.eu/Libraries/Documents/EU-US_Defence_Data_2010.sflb.ashx>.

[38] Lisbon Treaty, Article 42 (6), available at <www.lisbon-treaty.org/wcm/the-lisbon-treaty/treaty-on-european-union-and-comments/title-5-general-provisions-on-the-unions-external-action-and-specific-provisions-/chapter-2-specific-provisions-on-the-common-foreign-and-security-policy/section-2-provisions-on-the-common-security-and-defence-policy/129-article-42.html>.

[39] Guillaud hearing, Sénat.

[40] *Le Monde*, March 31, 2011.

[41] Guillaud hearing, Sénat.

[42] The November 2010 "Lancaster House" documents include "UK-France Summit 2010 Declaration on Defence and Security Co-operation," "Treaty Between the United Kingdom of Great Britain and Northern Ireland and the French Republic for Defence and Security Co-operation," and "Treaty Between the United Kingdom of Great Britain and Northern Ireland and the French Republic Relating to Joint Radiographic/Hydrodynamics Facilities." The February 2012 statement is the "UK-France declaration on security and defence." Texts of the declarations and treaties are available at <www.number10.gov.uk>.

[43] "Declaration on Strengthening European Cooperation in Security and Defence," February 4, 2003, in *From Copenhagen to Brussels—European defence: core documents*, Chaillot Papers No. 67, vol. 4, compiled by Antonio Missorili (Paris: Institute for Security Studies, December 2003), available at <www.iss.europa.eu/uploads/media/cp067e.pdf>.

[44] For a more detailed description of the French intervention force, see White Book, 210–214; for British force, see "The Strategic Defence and Security Review and the National Security Strategy: Government Response to the Committee's Sixth Report of Session 2010–12," House of Commons Defence Committee, November 10, 2011.

[45] Etienne de Durand, "Entente or Oblivion: Prospects and Pitfalls of Franco-British Co-operation on Defence," *Future Defence Review,* Working Paper Number 8, Royal United Services Institute, September 2010.

[46] François Heisbourg, "The defence of Europe: Towards a new transatlantic division of responsibilities," in *All Alone? What U.S. retrenchment means for Europe and NATO,* ed. Tomas Valasek (London: Centre for European Reform, February 2012).

[47] Etienne de Durand.

[48] Minister for the Armed Forces Nick Harvey, speech at the Franco-British Council Defence Co-operation Conference, March 31, 2011, available at <www.mod.uk>.

[49] Avis, Assemblée nationale, présenté au nom de la Commission de la défense nationale et des forces armées sur le projet de loi de finances pour 2012 (no. 3775), available at <www.assemblee-nationale.fr/13/budget/plf2012/a3809-tVII.asp>.

[50] House of Commons debate on Defence Treaties with France, November 2, 2010, Column 780, available at <www.publications.parliament.uk/pa/cm201011/cmhansrd/cm101102/debtext/101102-0001.htm>.

[51] Ibid.

[52] In July 1940, the British attacked a major part of the French fleet at Mers-el-Kebir (formerly French Algeria), killing over 1,200 French servicemen. France had signed an armistice with Germany 1 month earlier, and the British feared the French fleet would fall into German hands. During the 1982 Falklands war, Argentine aviation forces using French-made weapons systems sank four British ships, killing dozens of British personnel.

[53] Testimony of MBDA Chief Executive Officer Antoine Bouvier, Assemblée nationale, Commission de la défense nationale et des forces armées, May 18, 2011.

[54] Ibid.

[55] According to the February 17, 2012, summit declaration, the countries will jointly fund a contract led by Dassault Aviation (France) and BAE Systems (United Kingdom).

[56] France's presidential election takes place in two rounds; a first round with multiple candidates takes place on April 22, 2012, and the two candidates with the highest vote totals face off May 6. For the National Assembly elections, the two rounds take place on June 10 and 17.

[57] François Hollande, speech on national defense, March 11, 2012, available at <http://francoishollande.fr/dossiers/defense-armee-militaire-propositions>.

[58] President Sarkozy's news conference with Afghan President Hamid Karzai, January 27, 2012, available at <www.elysee.fr/president/les-actualites/conferences-de-presse/2012/conference-de-presse-de-mm-nicolas-sarkozy-et.12898.html>.

[59] The Socialists have scored a wave of electoral victories at the municipal and regional levels in recent years, and they won control of the Senate—whose members are elected indirectly—in 2011.

[60] Jean-Dominique Merchet, "Défense: pourquoi François Hollande opte pour le consensus national," *Secret défense*, January 15, 2012, available at <www.marianne2.fr/blogsecretdefense/Defense-pourquoi-Francois-Hollande-opte-pour-le-consensus-national_a483.html>.

[61] Hollande speech.

[62] Boeing Corporation and EADS engaged in a high-profile, multiyear competition for the U.S. Air Force contract to build 179 tanker aircraft. Boeing won the contract, estimated to be worth over $30 billion, in February 2011.

[63] See November 2010 "Lancaster House" documents, especially "UK-France Summit 2010 Declaration on Defence and Security Co-operation;" see also description of UK-French Bilateral Armament Cooperation, available at <www.ambafrance-uk.org/Defence-Procurement-Attache>.

[64] DOD, *Sustaining U.S. Global Leadership*.

[65] "Libyan air ops showcase French, UK, US partnership," *Jane's Defence Weekly*, March 21, 2012.

[66] House of Commons debate.

[67] Ibid. For an excellent overview of this subject, see Bruno Tertrais, "U.S.-French Nuclear Cooperation: Stretching the Limits of National Strategic Paradigms," James Martin Center for Nonproliferation Studies, July 26, 2011, available at <http://cns.miis.edu/wmdjunction>.

[68] Matthew Harries, "Britain and France as Nuclear Partners," *Survival* 54, no. 1 (February–March 2012).

[69] See "CSIS European Trilateral Track 2 Nuclear Dialogues Statement: Toward an Appropriate Mix of Conventional, Nuclear, and Missile Defense Forces," Center for Strategic and International Studies, August 24, 2011, available at <http://csis.org/files/publication/110824_European_Trilat_Appropriate_Mix_Statement.pdf>.

[70] Jean-Patrick Gaviard and Marc-Henri Figuier, "Reprenons l'initiative stratégique," *Le Monde*, February 14, 2012.

About the Author

Leo G. Michel is a Distinguished Research Fellow in the Center for Strategic Research, Institute for National Strategic Studies, at the National Defense University. Mr. Michel concentrates on transatlantic defense relations. He served previously in the Office of the Secretary of Defense where he was Director for North Atlantic Treaty Organization Policy, Director for Non-Nuclear Arms Control, Deputy U.S. Representative to the U.S.-Russia Bilateral Consultative Commission, and Deputy Director for Verification Policy. Before joining the Department of Defense, Mr. Michel worked in the Central Intelligence Agency's Directorate for Intelligence. He worked as a legislative assistant for national security affairs for a Member of Congress from 1975 to 1977 and served as a U.S. Navy officer from 1969 to 1972. Mr. Michel was promoted to the Senior Executive Service in 2000. He holds a Master of Arts degree from the Johns Hopkins School for Advanced International Studies and Bachelor of Arts degree from Princeton University.